THE WORDS OF
DESMOND TUTU

THE WORDS OF

DESMOND TUTU

SELECTED BY

NAOMI TUTU

Newmarket Press
New York

Library of Congress Cataloging-in-Publication Data

Tutu, Desmond.
    The words of Desmond Tutu.

    Bibliography: p.
    1. Tutu, Desmond—Quotations.   I. Tutu, Naomi.
II. Title.
BX5700.6.Z8T875   1989   283'.68   88-34567

First edition

To the next generation, especially Talesa and Xabiso—
may your struggle be one of building
and not tearing down.

CONTENTS

INTRODUCTION

How does one go about introducing the thoughts and words of one's father? Initially it appeared to me that this introduction would be the easiest part of compiling this book. After all, I have known him for nearly thirty years and have heard him speak and preach more than most. However, as I prepared to write the introduction and thought about the selections, it became obvious that the task was going to be much more complicated. This is mainly because, though I have intellectually accepted him as Archbishop Tutu, Nobel Peace Prize recipient, emotionally he is and always will be my *Tata*, first and foremost. While a handful of people might be reading this because they want to know Naomi's *Tata*, that is not who I am asked to introduce. Rather, I am introducing a man who has come to symbolize for many around the world the nonviolent struggle against apartheid.

THE WORDS OF DESMOND TUTU

What is it that takes the son of a schoolteacher and washerwoman from the townships of South Africa and a life as a parish priest, and makes him a world figure? I think the key is the priesthood, and that is where it is best for me to begin. It is easiest for me to start there because that is a role he has had all my life and it is also the most honest because, as you will see in this book, he considers himself a Christian and a priest above all. That is what guides his words and actions.

Almost all the sayings collected in this book refer in some way to Desmond Tutu's faith. This is through no conscious effort on my part; in fact, I struggled to find more that did not. But almost all the addresses and speeches I selected from, to diverse audiences and in a wide range of situations, made some reference to faith, God, and the response they require of those who believe. In the same way his actions and statements in opposition to apartheid are based on this faith and the teachings of Christianity. If you attempt to understand the man, his words, or his actions divorced from this faith, they have no meaning. Even the ambiguities about him, such as the abhorrence of violence but the belief that it might, in some circumstances, be the lesser of the two evils, are the result of his beliefs. He himself says over and over again he is forced by his faith to speak out against injustice and oppression. As he says in *Why We Must Oppose Apartheid,* "My passionate opposition to the evil and pernicious policy of apartheid has nothing to do with a political or any other ideology. It has everything to do with my faith as a Christian and my understanding of the imperatives of the gospel of Jesus Christ." And again in his reply to the State President P.W. Botha's question published in periodicals in South Africa and the world on who he is guided by in his opposition to the South African government, "My theological position derives from the Bible and from the teachings of the Church, both of which predate Marxism and the African National Congress by several centuries."

The role that my father plays in South Africa is, I believe, the role he thinks the Church must play throughout the world. In South Africa the role of the Church as critic of social and economic systems is made simpler because the injustice is so blatant. (In fact he has said on numerous occasions that it is almost easier to be a Christian in a situation of oppression.) However, this should be the Church's role in all societies, for nowhere is there a place where all people are living in peace and security. Christian peace is not simply the absence of conflict, but rather the presence of justice, reconciliation, fullness of life, health and well-being for all people. No country has achieved this, no country can achieve it in isolation, and it is the Church's role to encourage all people to strive for this, the true peace. The Church must be a constant critic of all forms of government until this is achieved.

Having listened to my father speak fairly often, my mother, sisters, and I now murmur to each other, "Speech number 14," or 21, or whatever number once he has started a presentation or sermon. He himself has stated on numerous occasions that he is very repetitive, because, he insists, he has only one fundamental message—the importance of community and respect for others. In his eyes, once we have all recognized this and have chosen to live by it, the world will be a better place.

It is interesting that these themes are of the utmost importance in the two systems that are his foundation, Christianity and African culture. A solitary Christian is a contradiction in terms as is, in African culture, a solitary human being. We are only Christians in our caring for and sharing with others, and we are human through our relationships with other human beings. So in Xhosa we say *U muntu ngu muntu ngabantu,* meaning a person is a person through other people. It is a call to respect others as part of ourselves, others on whom we rely in some way or another. Likewise, in Christianity we are one body and no part of the body can be unaffected by the pain or loss of another. But as we share each other's pain, so do we share each other's joy.

Thus, for my father, the Nobel was not *his* prize, but the prize of so many in South Africa and around the world who are part of the fight for a better society. In practical terms this led to some headaches for the organizers of the Nobel prize-giving ceremony in 1984, because my father insisted that representatives of all those who had assisted him in some way be present in Oslo. In the end his party consisted of people from around the world, from Terry Waite, the Archbishop of Canterbury's special envoy, to the Dean of General Seminary in New York where he had been when he was notified of his selection, to a contingent from the South African Council of Churches. The full party must have numbered at least forty, which was a blessing when, after a bomb scare during the presentation, the orchestra did not return and we were called upon to supply the music! The real importance of this crowd, however, was the statement it made of our need for one another in all situations, and that no one person no matter how gifted can achieve anything alone.

Rather than gifted, I think my father would consider himself blessed. Blessed in the people he has met throughout his life, from Bishop Trevor Huddleston, who showed him that respect is something due to others no matter the color of their skin or their situation in life, to my mother who taught him that a certain irreverence in life is necessary if you are to remain sane and enjoy life to its fullest.

All the above seems to paint a picture of a humorless, all-suffering human being, but the one thing most everyone who has heard my father speak comments on is his sense of humor. Even when talking about the insanity of apartheid to those who suffer it daily, he is able to draw laughter by comparing the basing of rights on skin color to basing them on the size of one's nose, as he has a fairly large one. There is some truth to the theory that he laughs and tries to get others to do so to stop himself from crying. However, I think there is also the realization that no situation is completely devoid of any joy or hope, for once that becomes true, then there is no reason to struggle or live. In addition, he believes that humor is liberating because once you begin to take yourself or your situation in life too seriously, you become a prisoner of your self-perception. That is one of the things that he believes the majority of white South Africans are guilty of. They have taken to heart the belief that they are innately superior to blacks and are therefore afraid of what would happen once they gave an inch and accepted our humanity. They are afraid that this would result in us doing to them what they have done to us but with vengeance. So he asks black South Africans to understand this fear while urging white South Africans to release themselves from it by taking those first steps towards a free South Africa. Not an easy role to play by any stretch of the imagination, because whites continue to vilify him as a trouble-maker, and many young blacks see people like him as standing in the way of liberation, so that I wonder if he would ever be able again to stop a crowd from killing a suspected informer as he did a few years ago. It seems more likely that the anger would be turned on him instead.

It is strange to hear the South African government and its supporters speak of my father as one who encourages violence and hate. If there is anybody I know who finds it impossible to hate another human being it is he. On many occasions I have felt frustrated by his attempts to teach us that hating someone else is hating ourselves and God. I finally decided it was impossible to change his view in 1982. I was to be married on July 3rd and on June 16th my fiancé, my sisters, and I went with my father to a service to commemorate those young people killed in the Soweto uprising of 1976. After the service, he left the churchyard, which was surrounded by police, to try to ensure that people were able to leave peacefully. A contingent of police stormed into the churchyard chasing some young people. My fiancé Corbin tried to intervene when three police then began to attack the parish priest— so they turned on us. When they were through, Corbin's glasses were broken and he had *sjambok* marks on his head and face while my arm was bleeding and my back was throbbing. When we got home, I asked my father, "Can you still ask us to forgive? Can you still believe they are our brothers, that we have some responsibility to them?" He had no profound statement that will be remembered for generations, but simply said, "I cannot ask you to do anything since you were the one beaten, but I can hope that if I am ever the one, I will still be able to forgive and pray for them. That is the strength I ask for."

Throughout this introduction, I have spoken of the importance of his faith to my father. Perhaps what is strangest about it is that he came by most of it after he decided to become a priest. Growing up, I knew my parents had been married in the Catholic church, so how did we end up as Anglicans? I decided, rather romantically, that married and with two children, my father had been dramatically called by God to the priesthood and therefore became an Anglican. I later found out that upon leaving teaching after the introduction of Bantu Education, he chose the priesthood rather as another form of service close in many ways to that of a teacher. But however he considers the decision at the time, I still believe that he was "called" because it is unlikely that he would have the strength to continue the struggle, or even to be able to survive, without his faith. He is too easily hurt and too needing of love to thrive in the position he now holds within South Africa without this anchor. A Desmond Tutu without his belief in an all loving, all forgiving God who created us for his purposes could not play the role he plays today. He *is* his faith, and it is his faith that sustains him and has made him what he is.

I hope these words will give to some a better understanding of my father's faith, and more importantly, of the part that the struggle against apartheid is playing in the greater struggle for a world governed by true peace.

—Naomi Tutu
London
December, 1988

FAITH
AND
RESPONSIBILITY

"The word of God calls his people to work for justice, for only thus can there be peace."

"The church must be ready to speak the truth in love. It has a responsibility for all, the rich and the poor, the ruler and the ruled, the oppressed and the oppressor, but it needs to point out that God *does* take sides. Incredibly, he sides with those whom the world would marginalize, whom the world considers of little account. That was what he did in the founding of Israel. He took their side when they did not deserve it against the powerful, against pharoah. That was a paradigmatic act that gave an important clue about the sort of God he is."

"One day at a party in England for some reason we were expected to pay for our tea. I offered to buy a cup for an acquaintance. Now he could have said, "No, thank you." You could have knocked me down with a feather when he replied, "No, I won't be subsidized!" Well, I never! I suppose it was an understandable attitude. You want to pay your own way and not sponge on others. But it is an attitude that may have seemed to carry over into our relationship with God—our refusal to be subsidized by Him. It all stems very much from the prevailing achievement ethic which permeates our very existence. It is drummed into our heads, from our most impressionable days, that you must grind the opposition into the dust. We get so worked up that our children can become nervous wrecks as they are egged on to greater efforts by competitive parents. It has got to the stage where the worst sin in our society is to have failed.

"What a tremendous relief it should be, and has been to many, to discover that we don't need to prove ourselves to God. We don't have to do anything at all, to be acceptable to Him. That is what Jesus came to say, and for that He got killed. He came to say, 'Hey, you don't have to earn God's love. It is not a matter for human achievement. You exist because God loves you already. You are a child of divine love.' The Pharisees, the religious leaders of His day, they couldn't buy that . . . They thought Jesus was proclaiming a thoroughly disreputable God with very low standards—any Tom, Dick, and Harry, Mary and Jane would soon be jostling around with the prim and proper ones. Stupendously this was true; no, just part of the truth. Jesus was saying that the unlikely ones, those despised ones, the sinners, the prostitutes, the tax collectors, would in fact precede the prim and proper ones into the Kingdom of God. That really set the cat among some ecclesiastical pigeons, I can tell you.

"When a chap is in love, he will go out in all kinds of weather to keep an appointment with his beloved. Love can be demanding, in fact more demanding than law. It has its own imperatives—think of a mother sitting by the bedside of a sick child through the night, impelled only by love. Nothing is too much trouble for love."

"To ignore people of other faiths and ideologies in an increasingly plural society is to be willfully blind to what the scriptures say about Christian witness. We are severely impoverished if we do not encounter people of other faiths with reverence and respect for their belief and integrity."

"The heart of the Christian Gospel is precisely that God the all holy One, the all powerful One is also the One full of mercy and compassion. He is not a neutral God inhabiting some inaccessible Mount Olympus. He is a God who cares about his children and cares enormously for the weak, the poor, the naked, the downtrodden, the despised. He takes their side not because they are good, since many of them are demonstrably not so. He takes their side because He is that kind of God, and they have no one else to champion them."

"An authentic Christian spirituality is utterly subversive to any system that would treat a man or woman as anything less than a child of God. It has nothing to do with ideology or politics. Every praying Christian, every person who has an encounter with God, must have a passionate concern for his or her brother and sister, his or her neighbor. To treat anyone of these as if he were less than the child of God is to deny the validity of one's spiritual experience."

"If we are to say that religion cannot be concerned with politics then we are really saying that there is a substantial part of human life in which God's writ does not run. If it is not God's then whose is it? Who is in charge if not the God and Father of our Lord Jesus Christ?

"Is it not interesting just how often people and churches are accused of mixing religion with politics?—almost always whenever they condemn a particular social political dispensation as being unjust. If the South African Council of Churches were to say now that it thought apartheid was not so bad, I am as certain as anything that we would not find ourselves where we are today. Why is it not being political for a religious body or a religious leader to *praise* a social political dispensation?"

"My passionate opposition to apartheid stems from my understanding of the Bible and the Christian faith. If anyone can prove that apartheid is consistent with the teachings of the Bible and Jesus Christ then I will burn my Bible and cease forthwith to be a Christian. Praise to God that no one can do that."

"It is interesting to note that many who have been Christian activists, such as St. Francis of Assisi, who went on a crusade and was deeply concerned with the poor and downtrodden, and St. Teresa of Avila, the Spanish nun who reorganized her Carmelite religious community, were people who put first things first. St. Francis is known to have spent a whole night in prayer enraptured as he repeated over and over again the phrase 'My God and my all,' and you recall that after a lengthy Lenten period of fasting and meditation he emerged from his cave bearing the marks of the nails of Christ in his hands and the wound in his side—the stigmata.

"All I am saying is that the Bible and our faith and its tradition declare unequivocally that for an authentic Christian existence the absolute priority must be spirituality. A church that does not pray is quite useless. Christians who do not pray are of no earthly worth. We must be marked by a heightened God consciousness. Then all kinds of things will happen."

"If you take your Christianity seriously you can't support apartheid, for Christianity and apartheid are totally incompatible. That is what our church and others are saying when they declare apartheid a heresy."

"Let me warn the government again: You are not God. You may be powerful, but you are mortal. Beware when you take on the church of God. Emperor Nero, Hitler, Amin, and many others have tried it and ended ignominiously. Get rid of apartheid, and we will have a new South Africa that is just, nonracial, and democratic, where black and white can exist amicably side by side in their home country as members of one family, the human family, God's family."

"True Christian worship includes the love of God and the love of neighbour. The two must go together or your Christianity is false. St. John asks in his first epistle how you can say you love God, whom you have not seen, if you hate your brother, whom you have. Our love for God is tested and proved by our love for our neighbour. This is what the churches, and perhaps especially the South African Council of Churches, attempt to do in that beautiful but sadly unhappy land which is South Africa."

"Jesus was quite categorical in expressing solidarity with those he called the least of his brethren: the naked, the hungry, the thirsty, the sick, the imprisoned. To act with compassion toward these is to act with compassion toward Jesus himself. In Isaiah 61 Jesus summed up the nature of his ministry:

> The spirit of the Lord is upon me, because he has anointed me to preach good news to the poor. He has sent me to proclaim release to the captives and recovering of sight to the blind, to set at liberty those who are oppressed.

"If we are the representatives of God, we must take sides. We have no choice really. To be neutral in a situation of injustice is to have chosen sides already. It is to support the status quo. We must look to our Lord and Master who is our peace.

"I would hope we could show our solidarity with those who are uprooted, that we would walk through the squalor of the slums, which are the result of deliberate government policy, that we would attend those horrific funerals, that we would be at the treason trials with the families of the detained. I know we do many of these things already. That is where we must be."

"We who have the privilege of working in situations of injustice and oppression, where God's children have their noses rubbed in the dust daily and their God-given human dignity is trodden callously underfoot with a cynical disregard for their human rights, are filled with an anamolous exhilaration. We are filled with an indomitable hope and exhilaration because we know that ultimately injustice and oppression and evil and exploitation cannot prevail and that the kingdoms of this world are becoming the kingdom of our God and his Christ.

"In a setting that claims we are made for alienation, separation, dividedness, hostility, and war, we must, as the church of God, proclaim that we are made for togetherness, for fellowship, for community, for oneness, for friendship, and peace. In a situation of injustice, oppression, and exploitation, we must proclaim that the justice and righteousness and equity of God will prevail. In a place where truth is a constant casualty, with many in high places taking loosely the demands of verity and truthfulness, we must declare that truth matters and that a people who have become immoral are in grave danger of collapse. In a situation where human life seems dirt cheap, with people being killed as easily as one swats a fly, we must proclaim that people matter and matter enormously, because they are created in the image of God. We must proclaim that apartheid must go and that a new dispensation will take its place, a dispensation where black and white will live together as members of one family, the human family, God's family."

"Christians from all over the world form a tremendous variety and rich diversity. How I have longed for my compatriots to experience a World Christian Conference–sponsored ecumenical event just to glory in the wonderful variety of people God has united in the *koinonia* of His Son's body—people from bewilderingly different ethnic, cultural, geographical, social, economic, and ecclesiastical backgrounds and yet remarkably able to confess Jesus Christ as Lord to the glory of the Father.

"You really cannot describe the texture of these gatherings at which you catch a glimpse of the true *oikumene*. There are tall people, short people, clever people (most seem so) and others not so clever, fat people, lean people, black, yellow, Caucasian people in a splendidly variegated array of national costumes and speaking a veritable Babel of languages, all (or nearly all) able to worship together, to receive the body and blood of our Lord and Savior together and all able to understand one another because of the marvel of simultaneous translation. You realized what God intended the church to be, a first fruit of the redeemed, a sign of hope that God intends us to be a family."

"My passionate opposition to the evil and pernicious policy of apartheid has nothing to do with a political or any other ideology. It has everything to do with my faith as a Christian and my understanding of the imperatives of the gospel of Jesus Christ. My opposition is based firmly and squarely on the Bible and on the injunctions of the Christian gospel. I have yet to hear the oppressed say, 'Archbishop Tutu, you are too political.' If anything, they will probably declare that we are not political enough. If I were to stand up here and say that I don't think apartheid to be too bad, then none of my erstwhile critics would accuse me of that heinous crime of mixing religion with politics."

APARTHEID

"I come from a beautiful land, richly endowed by God with wonderful resources, wide expanses, rolling mountains, singing birds, bright shining stars out of blue skies, with radiant sunshine, golden sunshine. There is enough of the good things that come from God's bounty; there is enough for everyone, but apartheid has confirmed some in their selfishness, causing them to grasp greedily a disproportionate share, the lion's share, because of their power."

"Humans are of infinite worth intrinsically because they are created in God's image. Apartheid, injustice, oppression, exploitation are not only wrong; they are positively blasphemous because they treat the children of God as if they are less than His."

"Ours is a deeply polarized society. It is a house divided against itself, hagridden by fear, suspicion, division, hostility, alienation, characterized by violence, injustice, oppression, unrest, and yet also by compassion, caring, concern, courageous witness for the truth, refusal to compromise on principle by people of all races."

"You remember the story of the Zambian boasting to a South African about their minister of the navy. The South African scoffed: 'You are landlocked. How can you have a minister of the navy?' The Zambian retorted: 'Ah, but you claim to have a minister of justice.' "

"I visited one of the banned people, Winnie Mandela. Her husband, Nelson Mandela, is serving a life sentence on Robben Island, our maximum security prison. I wanted to take her Holy Communion. The police told me I couldn't enter her house. So we celebrated Holy Communion in my car in the street in Christian South Africa. On a second occasion I went to see her on a weekend. Her restriction order is more strict on weekends.

She can't leave her yard. So we celebrated Holy Communion again in the street. This time Winnie was on one side of the fence and I was on the other. This in Christian South Africa in 1978."

"The consequence of sin is to divide, to break up, to cause to disintegrate, to separate, to alienate, to split apart. Apartheid partakes of this centrifugal nature of sin for it is in fact the essence of sin to separate. That is why we have said that apartheid is fundamentally, in its very nature, evil, immoral, and un-Christian."

"Let us all identify the problem. It is not Soviet expansionism, even if the Russians may have their eyes on our lucrative natural resources. The enemy is not the agitator. Let him try telling denizens of the affluent suburbs that they are suffering and oppressed and see how far he can get with that. The enemy is not 'out there.' It is not on the border. It is not an interfering hostile world. The enemy is right here. The enemy is apartheid, which has turned this country into the pariah of the world."

"For us blacks, the victims of apartheid, the declaration of a state of emergency is merely making *de jure* what has been *de facto*, because we have, in the black community, been living in a virtual state of emergency. We have been accustomed over the years to having meetings banned and community leaders detained. We have been used over the years to our leaders being tried for high treason or muzzled in some way or another, with quite extraordinary bail conditions imposed."

"A person banned for three or five years becomes a non-person, who cannot be quoted during the period of her banning order. She cannot attend a gathering, which means more than one person. Two persons together talking to a banned person are a gathering! She cannot attend the wedding or funeral of even her own child without special permission. She must be at home from 6:00 P.M. of one day to 6:00 A.M. of the next and on all public holidays, and from 6:00 P.M. on Fridays until 6:00 A.M. on Mondays for three years. She cannot go on holiday outside the magisterial area to which she has been confined. She cannot go to the cinema, nor to a picnic. That is severe punishment, inflicted without the evidence allegedly justifying it being made available to the banned person, not having it scrutinized in a court of law. It is a serious erosion and violation of basic human rights, of which blacks have precious few in the land of their birth."

"It won't do to tinker with this system. It cannot be reformed. It must be dismantled. It must be destroyed so that a new South Africa can rise."

"Apartheid has decreed the politics of exclusion. Seventy-three percent of the population is excluded from any meaningful participation in the political decision-making process of the land of their birth. . . . Blacks are expected to exercise their political ambitions in unviable, poverty-stricken, arid, Bantustan homelands, ghettoes of misery, inexhaustible reservoirs of cheap black labor, Bantustans into which South Africa is being balkanized. Blacks are systematically being stripped of their South African citizenship and being turned into aliens in the land of their birth. This is apartheid's Final Solution, just as Nazism had its Final Solution for the Jews in Hitler's Aryan madness."

"Detention without trial is an abrogation of the rule of law; it is a subverting of justice. It is to punish someone and to punish him severely without the inconvenience of having to prove his guilt in an open court. It is a very handy device greatly beloved of totalitarian, repressive governments."

"When a priest goes missing and is subsequently found dead, the media in the West carry his story in very extensive coverage. I am glad that the death of one person can cause so much concern. But in the same week that this priest is found dead, the South African police kill 24 blacks who had been participating in a protest, and 6,000 blacks are sacked for being similarly involved, and you are lucky to get that much coverage. Are we being told something I do not want to believe, that we blacks are expendable and that blood is thicker than water, that when it comes to the crunch you cannot trust whites, that they will club together? I don't want to believe that is the message being conveyed to us."

"It won't help the antisanctions lobby to vilify me. Even if they were to liquidate me, what I say is true: apartheid is filthy, it is vile, it is immoral, it is violent, it is vicious, it is evil, it is un-Christian. Even if I am not there, even if I can be shown to be a scoundrel of the first water, it won't help to change the nature of apartheid. Apartheid is the problem and the world agrees with us."

"Apartheid cannot survive without an enemy and so apartheid has to create enemies. If they are not external enemies, then they must be internal enemies."

"Apartheid says our value resides in a biological attribute, in this instance, skin color. A particular skin color is by definition not a universal phenomenon possessed by all human beings. The Bible, on the other hand, declares that what makes each and every person of infinite, incalculable worth is not this or that biological attribute. It is the fact that we are each created in the image of God."

"Only those who have been victims of oppression and injustice and discrimination know what I am talking about when I say that the ultimate evil is not the suffering, excruciating as that may be, which is meted out to those who are God's children. The ultimate evil of oppression, and certainly of that policy of South Africa called apartheid, is when it succeeds in making a child of God begin to doubt that he or she is a child of God."

VIOLENCE
AND
NONVIOLENCE

"Stability and peace in our land will not come from the barrel of a gun, because peace without justice is an impossibility."

"There is no peace in South Africa. There is no peace because there is no justice. There can be no real peace and security until there is first justice enjoyed by all inhabitants of that beautiful land. The Bible knows nothing about peace without justice, for that would be crying 'peace, peace,' where there is no peace. God's Shalom, peace, involves inevitable righteousness, justice, wholesomeness, fullness of life, participation in decision making, goodness, laughter, joy, compassion, sharing, and reconciliation."

"There will be more and more political harassment, bannings and detention, but these will not deter those who are determined to become free. The international community must make up its mind whether it wants to see a peaceful resolution of the South African Crisis or not. If it does, then let it apply pressure (diplomatic, political, but above all economic) on the South African Government to persuade them to go to the negotiating table with the authentic leaders of all sections of the South African population before it is too late."

"We are preparing for a society that is going to be able to discriminate between good and bad, and we must not allow ourselves to become like the system we oppose. We cannot afford to use methods of which we will be ashamed when we look back, when we say, '*Ja, magtag,* we shouldn't have done that.'

"We must remember, my friends, that we have been given a wonderful cause, the cause of freedom! And you and I must be those who will walk with heads held high. We will say, 'We used methods that can stand the harsh scrutiny of history.' "

"The paradigms that we've got to follow are biblical paradigms. Moses went to see the Pharoah not once but several times. Who are we to prejudge the grace of God. It's very difficult for me as a church leader to say, 'Go to hell,' to say God's grace cannot operate on P. W. Botha."

"Many are beginning to think the only way forward is the way of armed struggle. But I am certain that if we were to say today the government is serious about dismantling apartheid most people would be glad. None of our people is really bloodthirsty. They just want their place under the sun, a place where they are acknowledged for what they are—human beings made in the image of God."

"We must recognize that apartheid is the primary violence in South Africa. It's the violence of the migratory labor system, the violence of detention without trial, the violence that forces children to starve, the violence that stunts intellectual and spiritual growth. Apartheid is an evil and immoral system that must be destroyed."

"I am opposed to both the violence of those who main-
tain an unjust system and the violence of those who seek
to overthrow it. The important point to make is that many
people think violence is something that is going to be
introduced from the outside by the so-called terrorists, the
people of the liberation movements. The situation in
South Africa is already a violent one. It is the institutional violence, the structural violence of apartheid, that
has caused the answering violence of the liberation movements."

"When blacks—after many years during which their cau-
tious protest was consistently ignored—in desperation
opted for armed struggle, whites dubbed them 'terrorists,' which meant they could be ruthlessly imprisoned, hanged, or shot. The will to be free is not, however,
defeated by even the worst kind of violence. Such repressive violence has only succeeded in throwing South Africa
into a low-intensity civil war. Already South Africans
are staring at fellow South Africans through gunsights."

"I will never tell someone to pick up a gun. But I will pray for the man who picks up the gun, pray that he will be less cruel than he might otherwise have been, because he is a member of the community. We are going to have to decide: if this civil war escalates, what is our ministry going to be?"

"I am a lover of peace and I try to work for justice because only thus do I believe we can ever hope to establish durable peace. It is self-defeating to justify a truce based on unstable foundations of oppression. Such a truce can only be inherently unstable, requiring that it be maintained by institutional violence."

"International action and international pressure are among the few nonviolent options left. Yet how strident is the opposition to economic sanctions. Blacks cannot vote. We are driven therefore to invoke a nonviolent method that we believe is likely to produce the desired result. If this option is denied us, what then is left? If sanctions should fail, there is no other way but to fight."

"The problem is not sanctions. The problem is apartheid. I want apartheid destroyed, not reformed. If it can be done away without sanctions I will sing Alleluia. The onus is still on those who oppose sanctions to provide us with a viable nonviolent alternative."

"When a clash occurs between the laws of man and the laws of God, then for the Christian there can be no debate or argument about which he must obey. Our Lord told those who questioned Him: "Render unto Caesar the things that belong to Caesar and render unto God the things that belong to God." Caesar is God's servant to ensure that good and just order prevail. He cannot claim absolute authority without becoming blasphemous.

"We are a normally law-abiding people, but when the honor of God is at stake, we will disobey iniquitous and unjust laws. Please let us be mindful of the important distinction between what is legal and what is morally right."

"My father used to say 'Don't raise your voice. Improve your argument.' Good sense does not always lie with the loudest shouters, nor can we say that a large unruly crowd is always the best arbiter of what is right."

"All violence is evil, but a time may come when you have to decide between two evils—oppression or a violent overthrow of the oppressive regime. This happened in World War II. Did you allow Hitler to put children into gas ovens unhindered or did you go to war to stop him? Which was the lesser evil? Did you accept the tyranny of taxation without representation or did you fight the American War of Independence? Which was the lesser evil? I am sick and tired of those who would say that I support violence. I support the African National Congress in its aims to found a just, democratic, and nonracial South Africa, but I do not support its methods."

"Some of us, at great cost to our credibility, still talk about peaceful change in the face of escalating government intransigence and violence and growing impatience and frustration in the black community. We are seen especially by young blacks as standing in the way of revolution, and it is possible that whites may one day realize what we actually did and how much they owe to those whom they have most loved to hate, those whom they have delighted in seeing vilified and discredited."

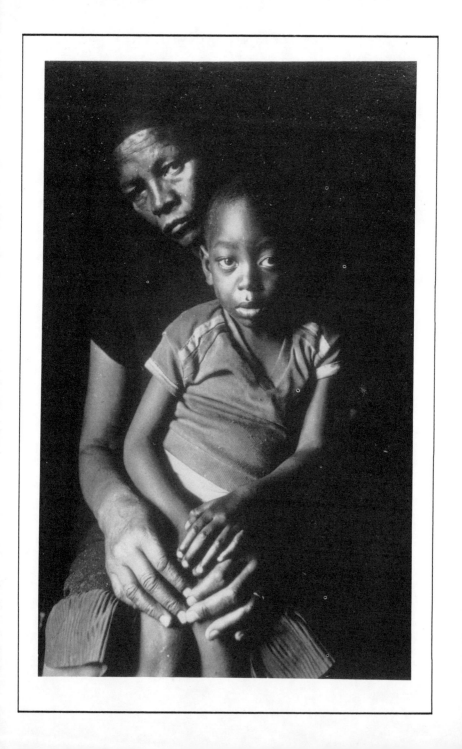

FAMILY

"A person is entitled to a stable community life, and the first of these communities is the family."

"Children are a wonderful gift. They are young and small persons, with minds and ideas, hating to be talked down to. They have an extraordinary capacity to see into the heart of things, and to expose sham and humbug for what they are. We must not idealize them too much, but I know that most of those I have had any dealings with respond wonderfully to being treated with respect, as persons who are responsible."

"Every day in a squatter camp near Cape Town, called K.T.C., the authorities have been demolishing flimsy plastic shelters that black mothers have erected because they were taking their marriage vows seriously. They have been reduced to sitting on soaking mattresses, with their household effects strewn round their feet, and whimpering babies on their laps, in the cold Cape winter rain. Every day the authorities have carried out these callous demolitions. What heinous crime have these women committed, to be hounded like criminals in this manner? All they have wanted is to be with their husbands, the fathers of their children. Everywhere else in the world they would be highly commended, but in South Africa, a land that claims to be Christian, and that boasts a public holiday called Family Day, these gallant women are treated so inhumanely, and yet all they want is to have a decent and stable family life. Unfortunately, in the land of their birth, it is a criminal offense for them to live happily with their husbands and fathers of their children. Black family life is thus being undermined, not accidentally, but by deliberate government policy. It is part of the price human beings, God's children, are called to pay for apartheid. An unacceptable price."

"The fulfillment of God's dream for human beings happens in the new dispensation when we are incorporated in Christ where 'there is neither Jew nor Gentile, slave nor free, male nor female, but we are all one in Christ.' Thus, it is not trying to be in vogue—to be climbing the latest bandwagon—to be concerned about the place of women in society and in the church. There can be no true liberation that ignores the question raised by the movement for the liberation of women."

"I believe that males and females have distinctive gifts, and both sets of gifts are indispensable for truly human existence. I am sure that the church has lost something valuable in denying ordination to women for so long. There is something uniquely valuable that women and men bring to the ordained ministry, and it has been distorted and defective as long as women have been debarred. Somehow men have been less human for this loss."

"There is something in the nature of God that corresponds to our maleness and our femaleness. We have tended to speak much more of the maleness, so we refer to the Fatherhood of God, which is as it should be. But we have missed out on the fullness that is God when we have ignored that which corresponds to our femaleness. We have hardly spoken about the Motherhood of God, and consequently we have been the poorer for this."

"I would like to refer to one aspect—a tremendous quality that women have—which relates to a like quality in God. It is the faith women have in people. Take a child who is a cause of much frustration and disillusion in others. The mother of that child can see the beauty and goodness hidden deep down, and women are much more patient than men in trying to bring that goodness to the surface. They have the capacity, more than men, to cherish that good and bring it to fruition. Women, we need you to give us back our faith in humanity."

"The father leaves his family in the Bantustan homeland, there eking out a miserable existence, whilst he,
if he is lucky, goes to the so-called white man's town as
a migrant, to live an unnatural life in a single-sex hostel for eleven months there, being prey to drunkenness,
prostitution, and worse. . . . This cancer, eating away
at the vitals of black family life, is deliberate government
policy. It is part of the cost of apartheid, exorbitant in
terms of human suffering."

"In pursuance of apartheid's ideological racist dream, over
3,000,000 of God's children have been uprooted from
their homes, which have been demolished, whilst they have
been dumped in the Bantustan homeland resettlement
camps. . . . These dumping grounds are far from where
work and food can be procured easily. Children starve,
suffer from the often irreversible consequences of mal-
nutrition. . . . They starve in a land that could be the
breadbasket of Africa, a land that normally is an exporter
of food."

"We should be appalled that the world has a refugee population of over ten million people—not just statistics, but people who are mothers, fathers, children, husbands, wives to somebody. They are not just faceless digits but human persons for whom our Lord and Savior died. He identified fully with them as one who had himself been a refugee."

"Apartheid has spawned discriminatory education, such as Bantu education, education for serfdom, ensuring that the government spends only about one-tenth on one black child per annum for education what it spends on a white child. It is education that is decidedly separate and unequal. It is to be wantonly wasteful of human resources, because so many of God's children are prevented, by deliberate government policy, from attaining their fullest potential. South Africa is paying a heavy price already for this iniquitous policy because there is a desperate shortage of skilled manpower, a direct result of the short-sighted schemes of the racist regime. It is a moral universe that we inhabit, and good and right and equity matter in the universe of the God we worship. And so, in this matter, the South African government and its supporters are being hoisted with their own petard."

"Apartheid is upheld by a phalanx of iniquitous laws, such as the Population Registration Act, which decrees that all South Africans must be classified ethnically, and duly registered according to these race categories. Many times in the same family one child has been classified white whilst another with a slightly darker hue has been classified colored, with all the horrible consequences for the latter of being shut out from membership of a greatly privileged caste. There have, as a result, been several child suicides. This is too high a price to pay for racial purity."

"In one area of Soweto the youth erected barricades to stop the security forces from evicting those who refused to pay rent. The police went indiscriminately into homes in the area, ordered the children into the streets, and beat them. When the children ran away, they shot them. I went to one such home, where a thirteen-year-old boy had been shot dead. His younger brother, who had been shot in the stomach, was in critical condition in the hospital. The stunned mother sat silently in her chair. She kept wiping her eyes but there were no tears. I tried to talk to her about the love of God and silently asked, 'How long, oh Lord.' "

"Because there is global insecurity, nations are engaged in a mad arms race, spending billions of dollars wastefully on instruments of destruction, when millions are starving. Just a fraction of what is expended so obscenely on defense budgets would make the difference in enabling God's children to fill their stomachs, be educated, and given the chance to lead fulfilled and happy lives. We have the capacity to feed ourselves several times over, but we are daily haunted by the spectacle of the gaunt dregs of humanity shuffling along in endless queues, with bowls to collect what the charity of the world has provided, too little too late. God created us for fellowship. God created us so that we should form the human family, existing together because we were made for one another. We are not made for an exclusive self-sufficiency but for interdependence, and we break the law of being at our peril."

"Our children are being used as hostages in the power game of the government of South Africa. By controlling our children, the government hopes to control the parents. I am not just talking about black children, though they are by far the group that suffers the most. I speak also of white children, poor white youngsters who learn to hate at a very young age, who learn to salute, to march, to fear children with black skin, who are being trained in their bodies and their minds and their spirits to prepare for war."

"We of an older generation are on the whole still scared of arrest, of police dogs, of tear gas, of prison, and of death. But these young people are quite something else. They have experienced it all—yes, they have seen friends, brothers, and sisters die, and they are no longer scared. They are just determined. They are determined that they are going to be free, they and their reluctant, cowed parents. They have, they believe, sat for too long, listening night after night to the stories of their parents' daily humiliations just because they were black. They have decided that enough is enough. They are people with iron in their souls."

"My wife and I decided early on in our marriage that we were going to try to let our children do a lot of things that we had been denied in our childhood. We had been brought up to know that children are meant to be seen and not heard. So as children we used to feel so terribly frustrated when those gods of our household—our parents and their grown-up friends—were discussing something really interesting. We were burning to ask 'who' or 'what' in order to clarify some obscure point, but we never dared to interrupt.

"So we did not want our children to go through all those traumas. But it was not easy. I remember for instance saying to our youngest, who was then a very chirpy three-year-old, and quite sure that there were very few things that she did not know in the world: 'Mpho, darling, please keep quiet, you talk too much.' Do you think she was at all deflated by this rebuke? Not at all— quick as a shot she retorted: 'Daddy, you talk a lot too.'

"We stuck it out very painfully. We let them join in discussions with our adult friends—they interrupted, they argued, they contributed. We discovered there was much fun in the home, and we parents developed as we pitted our strengths against those of our children. They were persons in their own right, and we had to think out many things that previously we had taken for granted. I did not mean letting go of discipline, because a rebellious child is really testing out the parameters of acceptable conduct, and that is part of the painful process of growing up."

THE COMMUNITY—
BLACK AND WHITE

"One of the ways of helping to destroy a people is to tell them that they don't have a history, that they have no roots."

"Africans believe in something that is difficult to render in English. We call it *ubuntu, botho*. It means the essence of being human. You know when it is there and when it is absent. It speaks about humaneness, gentleness, hospitality, putting yourself out on behalf of others, being vulnerable. It embraces compassion and toughness. It recognizes that my humanity is bound up in yours, for we can only be human together."

"There is an old film called *The Defiant Ones*. In one
scene, two convicts manacled together escape. They fall
into a ditch with slippery sides. One of them claws his
way to near the top and just about makes it. But he
cannot. His mate to whom he is manacled is still at the
bottom and drags him down. The only way they can
escape to freedom is together. The one convict was black
and the other white: a dramatic parable of our situation
in South Africa. The only way we can survive is together,
black and white; the only way we can be truly human
is together, black and white."

"Large crowds are scurrying home past the cathedral on
their way to the main Johannesburg railway station; they
seem like so many ants. In the morning it is the same
story, only the traffic is in the opposite direction. Blacks
live more than twelve miles away, mainly in the twin city
of Soweto (abbreviation for South Western Township),
with nearly a million black inhabitants. They start from
home in the dark and return when the street lights

(where they have them) are on. They hardly see their children except over the weekend, and their transport is woefully inadequate, with dangerously overcrowded trams and buses."

"The black community can be dealt with effectively only through its recognized leaders. Anything else the government attempts will be like fiddling while the fires of revolution burn in our country."

"In our African language we say 'a person is a person through other persons.' I would not know how to be a human being at all except I learned this from other human beings. We are made for a delicate network of relationships, of interdependence. We are meant to complement each other. All kinds of things go horribly wrong when we break that fundamental law of our being. Not even the most powerful nation can be completely self-sufficient."

"We were meant to be as caring as a good farmer who tends the soil, not being unwantonly wasteful of irreplaceable natural resources and not behaving irresponsibly toward nature, polluting the air and water so recklessly."

"The African, on his side, regards the universe as one composite whole; an organic entity, progressively driving toward greater harmony and unity, whose individual parts exist merely as interdependent aspects of one whole realizing their fullest life in the corporate life where communal contentment is the absolute measure of values. His philosophy of life strives toward unity and aggregation, toward greater social responsibility."

"I understand why white people have the kind of perceptions that they have, which are totally different from the perceptions of blacks. If my wife and I had lived in the northern suburbs of Johannesburg always, what would we know about the state of emergency. I mean, you say to white people, 'We are in a state of emergency.' 'State of emergency? What state of emergency are you talking about?' What do they know about rubber bullets that shoot through their own children? What do they know about tear gas? What do they know about Caspirs, which rumble through our townships? State of emergency? We wake up on a Sunday in our northern suburban home. The salubrious, clean air, the breeze floating through the trees. . . . And I drive out of there with my wife, as we are going to Soweto. At nine o'clock we come to Soweto, and we have to put on our headlights because of the smog."

"People have been turned into aliens in the land of their birth, because aliens cannot claim any rights, least of all political rights. Millions have been deprived of their birthright, their South African citizenship; stable black communities have been destroyed, and those who have been uprooted have been dumped as you dump not people but things, in arid poverty-striken Bantustan homeland resettlement camps. Three and a half million people are treated in such a callous and heartless fashion in a land whose newest constitution invokes the name of God to sanctify a vicious, evil, and totally immoral and utterly un-Christian system, a system as evil, as immoral, as un-Christian as communism and Nazism."

"The university is dedicated to the pursuit of truth and imbued with a passion to follow the evidence wherever it might lead. Sadly, far too many of the institutions claiming to be universities in South Africa actually base themselves on a lie, which, if not consciously espoused, is acquiesced to by what those institutions do. The lie is that people should be separated because of fundamentally irreconcilable ethnic differences. How can you say that people are dedicated to the pursuit of truth when they have tried to provide intellectual respectability to this horrendous lie, which has caused so much unnecessary suffering to millions. A university must have a social conscience."

"We shall be free, all of us, black and white. Let us sit down together, black and white. I have said before and say again the minimum conditions for starting negotiations: lift the state of emergency; release detainees and political prisoners and allow exiles to return freely; unban political organizations; and then talk to those whom the people identify as their representatives and leaders. We shall be free only together, black and white. We shall survive only together, black and white. We can be human only together, black and white."

76

"I am black and there are many times when I have asked whether God really cared for us when I have looked at some of the things that our people have suffered. When the South African Defense Forces raided Maputo and Maseru a few years ago, we were told we could not hold memorial services. I held such services because I did not think then, nor do I think now, that I can be told by a secular authority what services I may or may not hold. They kill our children and then prescribe how we may bury them and they think we do not hurt. What do they think happens to us? For them we are really less than human, spoken of as 'those people.' Our pain, our anguish one day will burst forth in an unstoppable flood."

"White South Africans are not demons. White South Africans are ordinary human beings. Most of them are very scared human beings, and I ask the audience, 'Wouldn't you be scared if you were outnumbered five to one?'

"Now my brothers and sisters, let me tell you something. I am the bishop of the Diocese of Johannesburg. My flock is black, my flock is white. One has got to say to our people, 'I love you, I care for you, enormously.' And when I care about black liberation, it is because I care about white liberation."

"To the white community in general I say express your commitment to change by agreeing to accept a redistribution of wealth and a more equitable sharing of the resources of our land. Be willing to accept voluntarily a declension of your very high standard of living. Isn't it better to lose something voluntarily, and to assist in bringing about change—political power sharing—in an orderly fashion, rather than seeing this come about through bloodshed and chaos, when you stand to lose everything?"

"All of us [blacks worldwide] are bound to Mother Africa by invisible but tenacious bonds. She has nurtured the deepest things in us blacks. All of us have roots that go deep into the warm soil of Africa, so that no matter how long and traumatic our separation from our ancestral home has been, there are things we are often unable to articulate but which we feel in our very bones, things which make us different from others who have not suckled the breasts of our mother, Africa. Don't most of us, for instance, find the classical arguments for the existence of God just an interesting cerebral game, because Africa taught us long ago that life without belief in a supreme being was just too absurd to contemplate? And don't most of us thrill as we approach the awesomeness of the transcendent when many of our contemporaries find even the word God an embarrassment? How do you explain our shared sense of the corporateness of life, our rejection of Hellenistic dichotomies in our insistence that life, material and spiritual, secular and sacred, is all of a piece?"

"Unless we work assiduously so that all of God's children, our brothers and sisters, members of one human family, all will enjoy basic human rights, the right to a fulfilled life, the right of movement, the freedom to be fully human, within a humanity measured by nothing less than the humanity of Jesus Christ Himself, then we are on the road inexorably to self-destruction, we are not far from global suicide—and yet it could be so different."

TOWARD A NEW
SOUTH AFRICA

"I long and work for a South Africa that is more open and more just; where people count and where they will have equal access to the good things of life, with equal opportunity to live, work, and learn. I long for a South Africa where there will be equal and untrammeled access to the courts of the land, where detention without trial will be a thing of the hoary past, where bannings and other such arbitrary acts will no longer be even so much as mentioned, and where the rule of law will hold sway in the fullest sense. In addition, all adults will participate fully in political decision making, and in other decisions that affect their lives. Consequently, they will have the vote and be eligible for election to all public offices. This South Africa will have integrity of territory with a common citizenship, and all the rights and privileges that go with such a citizenship, belonging to all its inhabitants."

"If it weren't for faith, I would have given up long ago. I am certain lots of us would have been hate-filled and bitter. For me, the scriptures have become more and more thoroughly relevant to our situation. They speak of a God who, when you worship him, turns you around to be concerned for your neighbor. He does not tolerate a relationship with himself that excludes your neighbor."

"There is no such thing as separate freedom—freedom is indivisible. At the present time we see our white fellow South Africans investing much of their resources to protect their so-called separate freedoms and privileges. They have little time left to enjoy them as they check the burglar proofing, the alarm system, the gun under the pillow, and the viciousness of the watchdog. These resources could be employed in more creative ways to improve the quality of life of the entire community. Our white fellow South Africans think that their security lies in possessing a formidable and sophisticated arsenal of weapons. But they must know in their hearts that the security of all of us consists in a population whose members, black and white, are reasonably contented because they share equitably in the good things, which all, black and white, have cooperated to produce."

"We shall be free because our cause is a just cause. We do not want to dominate others, we just want to have our humanity acknowledged. Our freedom is not the gift of white people. They cannot decide to give or to with-hold it. Our freedom is an inalienable right bestowed on us by God."

"The award [the Nobel Prize] is a tremendous political statement. It says that despite all distortion of truth, the world recognizes that we are striving for peace. It is a tremendous affirmation that our cause is just and our methods are praiseworthy."

"The world is on our side—on the side of justice, of liberation, of South Africa, of South Africans, black and white who want a new South Africa. The world is not anti–South African, nor antiwhite (it would be odd for a white English person or American to be antiwhite). It is firmly and decidedly anti-apartheid, anti-oppression, anti-injustice, and the world knows that we are on the winning side."

"There are two things we need to say to our people: that the liberation is certain and it is going to be costly. I use this extraordinary vision in the Revelation of St. John the Divine. It's a vision of souls who have been killed during some persecution or other. And they are lying under the altar, and they are crying to the Lord. 'How long, Lord. How long is this thing going to go on?' And the extraordinary answer is not 'Don't worry, it will be all right.' The extraordinary answer is 'Wait a bit, because more of your brothers and sisters are going to die before the consummation.' "

"We believe that there can be no real peace in our beloved land until there is fundamental change. Please believe us when we say there is much goodwill left, although we have to add that time and patience are running out. We recognize that fundamental change cannot happen overnight, so we suggest that only four things need to be done to give real hope that this change is going to happen:

"1. Let the Government commit themselves to a common citizenship in an undivided South Africa. If this does not happen we will have to kiss a peaceful change good-bye.

"2. Please abolish the Pass Laws. Nothing is more hateful in a hateful system for blacks than these laws. I wish God could give me the words that could describe the dramatic change that would occur in relationships in this country if the real abolition of the Pass Laws were to happen.

"3. Please stop immediately all population removals and the uprooting of people. It is in my view totally evil and has caused untold misery.

"4. Set up a uniform educational system. We want to suggest that all universities be declared open and that the black universities be free to appoint blacks who have credibility in the black community. Otherwise we fear that unrest in these institutions will remain endemic.

"If these four things were done as a beginning, then we would be the first to declare out loud: please give the government a chance; they seem, in our view, to have embarked on the course of real change."

"Fundamentally, I believe history teaches us a categorical lesson: that once a people are determined to become free, then nothing can stop them from reaching their goal."

"God called Steve Biko to be his servant in South Africa—to speak up on behalf of God, declaring what the will of this God must be in a situation such as ours, a situation of evil, injustice, oppression, and exploitation. God called him to be the founding father of the Black Consciousness movement, against which we have had tirades and fulminations. Steve knew and believed fervently that being problack was not the same thing as being antiwhite. The Black Consciousness movement is not a 'hate white movement,' despite all you have heard to the contrary. He had a far too profound respect for persons as persons to want to deal with them under ready-made, shop-soiled categories.

"Steve has started something that is quite unstoppable. The powers of evil, of injustice, of oppression, of exploitation have done their worst and they have lost. They have lost because they are immoral and wrong, and our God, the God of Exodus, the liberator God, is a God of justice and righteousness, and he is on the side of justice and liberation and goodness. We thank and praise God for giving us such a magnificent gift in Steve Biko, and for his sake, and the sake of ourselves and our children, let us dedicate ourselves anew to the struggle for the liberation of our beloved land, South Africa."

"We need Nelson Mandela, because he is almost certainly going to be our first black prime minister. He represents all our genuine leaders, in prison and in exile. So to call for his release is really to say, please let us sit down, black and white together, each with our acknowledged leaders, and work out our common future so that we can move into this new South Africa, which will be filled with justice, peace, love, righteousness, compassion, and caring."

"We must demonstrate to the people of South Africa, both black and white, that the people of the world are not only watching, they are singing a new song, they are raising the trumpets of a new day. And their song will resonate around the world. And their song will break down the walls that isolate my people in their townships and in their hearts. I call for the reverberation of their song to free the hearts of my people, and to shift the tone of conversation and action forever."

"Nothing could have been deader than Jesus on the cross on that first Good Friday. And the hopes of his disciples had appeared to die with the crucifixion. Nothing could have been deeper than the despair of his followers when they saw their Master hanging on the cross like a common criminal. The darkness that covered the earth for three hours during that Friday symbolized the blackness of their despair.

"And then Easter happened. Jesus rose from the dead. The incredible, the unexpected, happened. Life triumphed over death, light over darkness, love over hatred, good over evil. That is what Easter means—hope prevails over despair. Jesus reigns as Lord of Lords and King of Kings. Oppression and injustice and suffering can't be the end of the human story. Freedom and justice, peace and reconciliation are His will for all of us, black and white, in this land and throughout the world. Easter says to us that despite everything to the contrary, His will for us will prevail, love will prevail over hate, justice over injustice and oppression, peace over exploitation and bitterness.

"The Lord is risen. Alleluia."

"If God be for us who could be against us?"

Acceptance of the Nobel Peace Prize
The Right Reverend Desmond Mpilo Tutu
Bishop of Johannesburg
Oslo, Norway, December 10, 1984

Your majesty, members of the Royal Family,
Mr. Chairman, Ladies and Gentlemen:

Many thousands of people round the world have been thrilled with the award of the Nobel Peace Prize for 1984 to Desmond Mpilo Tutu. I was told of a delegation of American churchpeople who were visiting Russia. On hearing the news they and their Russian hosts celebrated the Nobel Peace Prize Winner.

There has been a tremendous volume of greetings from heads of state, world leaders of the Christian church and other faiths as well as from so-called ordinary people—notable exceptions being the Soviet and South African governments.

The prize has given fresh hope to many in the world that has sometimes had a pall of despondency cast over it by the experience of suffering, disease, poverty, famine, hunger, oppression, injustice, evil and war—a pall that has made many wonder whether God cared, whether He was omnipotent, whether He was loving and compassionate. The world is in such desperate straits, in such a horrible mess that it all provides almost conclusive proof that a good and powerful and loving God such as Christians and people of other faiths say they believe in could not exist, or if He did He really could not be a God who cared much about the fate of His creatures or the world they happened to inhabit which seemed to be so hostile to their aspirations to be fully human.

I once went to a friend's house in England.

There I found a charming book of cartoons entitled *My God*. One showed God with appeals and supplications bombarding Him from people below and He saying, "I wish I could say, 'Don't call me, I'll call you.' " And another declared "Create in 6 days and have eternity to regret it."

My favourite shows God somewhat disconsolate and saying, "Oh dear, I think I have lost my copy of the divine plan." Looking at the state of the world you would be forgiven for wondering if He ever had one and whether He had not really botched things up.

New hope has sprung in the breast of many as a result of this prize—the mother watching her child starve in a Bantustan homeland resettlement camp, or one whose flimsy plastic covering was demolished by the authorities in the K.T.C. squatter camp in Cape Town; the man emasculated by the Pass Laws as he lived for 11 months in a single sex hostel; the student receiving an inferior education; the activist languishing in a consulate or a solitary confinement cell, being tortured because he thought he was human and wanted that God-given right recognised; the exile longing to kiss the soil of her much loved motherland, the political prisoner watching the days of a life sentence go by like the drip of a faulty tap, imprisoned because he knew he was created by God not to have his human dignity or pride trodden underfoot.

A new hope has been kindled in the breast of the millions who are voiceless, oppressed, dispossessed, tortured by the powerful tyrants; lacking elementary human rights in Latin America, in South East Asia, the Far East, in many parts of Africa and behind the Iron Curtain, who have their noses rubbed in the dust. How wonderful, how appropriate that this award is made today—December 10, Human Rights Day. It says more eloquently than anything else that this is God's world and He is in charge. That our cause is a just cause; that we will attain human rights in South Africa and everywhere in the world. We shall be free in South Africa and everywhere in the world.

I want to thank the Nobel Committee, I want to thank the Churches in Norway and everywhere for their support, their love and their prayers.

On behalf of all these for whom you have given new hope, a new cause for joy, I want to accept this award in a wholly representative capacity.

I accept this prestigious award on behalf of my family, on behalf of the South African Council of Churches, on behalf of all in my motherland, on behalf of those committed to the cause of justice, peace, and reconciliation everywhere.

If God be for us who can be against us?

CHRONOLOGY

1931
October

Tutu is born to Zachariah (a schoolteacher) and Aletha Malthare (a housewife) Tutu in Klerksdorp in the Western Transvaal.

1945–1950

Tutu attends the Johannesburg Bantu High School (Madibane) in Western Native Township.

1948

South Africa's National Party wins the national election on an apartheid platform, vowing to broaden and further institutionalize state racism.

1950

The National Party enacts some of the cornerstones of apartheid, including: the Population Registration Act, classifying all South Africans by race; and the Group Areas Act, enforcing racial segregation, uprooting blacks, "coloureds," and Indians from their communities and stripping them of their property.

1951–1953   Tutu attends the Pretoria Bantu Normal College, receiving a teacher's diploma.

1951   The Bantu Authorities Act, creating the "homelands" system, is enacted.

1952   The African National Congress wages the Defiance Campaign against the new apartheid laws.

1954   Tutu receives a BA from the University of South Africa, then teaches for a year at his old high school, Madibane.

1955
March   The government passes the Bantu Education Act, depriving all non-whites of an academic education. Tutu will eventually quit teaching as a result.

June   The Freedom Charter—the South African resistance's statement of principles—is drafted by 3,000 delegates assembled by the national Action Council of the Congress of the People.

July   Tutu marries Leah Nomalizo.

1955–1958   Tutu teaches at the Munsieville High School in Krugersdorp.

1958–1960   Tutu receives ordination training at St. Peter's Theological College in Johannesburg.

1960   South Africa's first black bishop, Alpheus Zulu, is consecrated.

March	The Sharpeville Massacre. Police kill 69 and wound 180 at a peaceful demonstration against pass laws. The government subsequently bans the ANC and the Pan-Africanist Congress.
December	Tutu is ordained as deacon.
1962	Nelson Mandela, leader of the ANC, is imprisoned on Robben Island.
1962–1966	The Tutu family lives in London, where Desmond Tutu is part-time curate at St. Alban's and receives BA honours and a Masters in Theology from King's College.
1966–1970	Tutu serves on the teaching staff of the Federal Theological Seminary, Alice.
1967	The Terrorism Act is passed, allowing police to detain suspects indefinitely.
1968	Steve Biko and others form the South African Student's Organization and spearhead the growing Black Consciousness Movement.
1970–1972	Tutu is lecturer in theology at the University of Botswana, Lesotho, and Swaziland.
1973	Steve Biko is banned.
1975	Tutu is named Dean of Johannesburg, thereby becoming the Anglican church's first black Dean. The family moves to Soweto rather than into the posh deanery in Johannesburg's "white's only" section.

1976
May

In his first public political initiative, Tutu sends an open letter to Prime Minister John Vorster appealing for an end to the homelands system and other reforms.

June

The Soweto Uprising. On June 16, 15,000 schoolchildren march in protest of Bantu education; over the next three weeks, 600 people—most of them students and schoolchildren—are killed.

July

Tutu is consecrated Bishop of Lesotho in St. Mary's Cathedral, Johannesburg.

1977
September

Steve Biko is killed by security police while in custody and buried in Kingwilliamstown. Tutu gives the funeral oration.

1978
March

Tutu becomes General Secretary of the South African Council of Churches.

September

P.W. Botha becomes Prime Minister after John Vorster resigns in scandal.

1979

Tutu is awarded an Honorary Doctorate of Law by Harvard University.

1980

The government confiscates Tutu's passport in reprisal for his call for an international boycott of South African coal.

May	Tutu becomes Rector of St. Augustine's, Orlando West in Soweto.
1982	Tutu is awarded the Honorary Doctorate of Sacred Theology by Columbia University.
1984 **October**	Tutu is awarded the Nobel Peace Prize. He had been nominated twice before.
November	Tutu is elected Bishop of Johannesburg, the Anglican Church of Southern Africa's second most important title after Archbishop of Cape Town.
1985 **March**	Police massacre 19 black demonstrators in Uitenhage during an increasingly turbulent year. 700 die in township unrest by September.
Spring	The divestment movement, begun at Columbia University, spreads throughout campuses and businesses in the United States.
July	The government declares a State of Emergency, subjecting citizens to arrest, imprisonment and torture without warrant.
1986	Tutu is awarded the Martin Luther King, Jr., Peace Award in Atlanta.
January	Tutu visits the U.S. and issues outspoken attacks on South Africa's State of Emergency.

April	Tutu calls for international economic sanctions against the apartheid regime, exposing himself to potential charges of treason.
June	After a brief respite, the State of Emergency is reimposed with even tighter restrictions on the public and the press.
September	Tutu is enthroned as Archbishop of Capetown.

1987

June	Tutu warns in Mozambique that black South Africans could be justified in taking up arms against an unjust government.
August	Tutu is elected President of the All African Conference of Churches.

1988

February	Tutu and other church leaders are arrested as they march on the South African Parliament to protest the banning of anti-apartheid organizations.
May	Tutu is awarded his 25th honorary doctorate by Northeastern University, Boston.
September	Tutu illegally urges South Africans to boycott apartheid municipal elections to be held in October. The government seizes a recording of his sermon, but backs down on threats to prosecute.
November	South African Angelican bishops give Tutu his strongest backing yet on his call for sanctions against apartheid.

SOURCES

Address given at a Home and Family Life Conference, Hammanskraal, 1979. (Home)

Address given at Natal University, 1980. (Natal I)

Address given at Natal University, 1981. (Natal II)

Address given at the University of the Western Cape, 1987. (UWC I)

Address given at the University of the Western Cape, 1988. (UWC II)

Address given in New York City, 1988. (New York)

Address on acceptance of the Nobel Peace Prize, 1984. (Nobel)

Address to the World Council of Churches Central Committee, Kingston, Jamaica, 1979. (Kingston)

Article dated November 8, 1978. (Article)

Article written for the African-America Institute, 1981. (AAI Article)

"Blessed are the meek for they shall inherit the earth," BBC Lent Series, 1988. (Lent)

"The Challenges of God's Mission," address to the United Methodists, Louisville, Kentucky, 1987. (Louisville)

"Change or Illusion," address to a Black Sash Conference, 1980. (Black Sash)

Charge delivered to the Episcopal Synod, 1987. (Charge)

Charge delivered to the Special Synod of the Archdiocese of Cape Town, 1987. (Special Synod)

"A Christian Vision of the Future of South Africa." (Christian Vision)

Christianity and Crisis, "Voices of South Africa." (Christianity and Crisis)

Crying in the Wilderness, by Desmond Tutu, Grand Rapids, Michigan: William B. Eerdmans Publishing Company, 1982. (Crying)

"Freedom Fighters or Terrorists." (Fighters)

Funeral Oration for Steve Biko, 1977. (Biko)

Hope and Suffering, by Desmond Tutu, Grand Rapids, Michigan, William B. Eerdmans Publishing Company, 1983. (Hope)

"Major contributions of the World Council of Churches over 40 Years—A Personal View." (WCC Article)

New York Times Magazine, 1988 (Times)

Presentation to the Eloff Commission of inquiry, 1982. (Eloff)

"Scape-Goatism," address given to the Cape Press Club, 1987. (Cape Press Club)

Sermon delivered on the feast of Epiphany, Kingston, Jamaica, 1979. (Epiphany)

Sermon delivered at St. George's Cathedral, 1987. (St. George)

Sermon delivered at St. George's Cathedral, Pentecost, 1987. (Pentecost)

"Speaking within the South African Context." (Context)

Tutu: Voice of the Voiceless, by Shirley de Boulay, Grand Rapids, Michigan: William B. Eerdmans Publishing Company, 1988. (Tutu)

Welcome to Gustav Gutierrez, 1988. (Welcome)

"Whither South Africa," address given at Woodstock Town Hall, 1985. (Woodstock)

"Why We Must Oppose Apartheid." (Oppose)

Following is a list of the above sources in order of their appearance within each section of the book. Sources are identified by the key words which appear in parentheses at the end of each citation.

FAITH AND RESPONSIBILITY: Context, Context, Natal II, WCC Article, Lent, Pentecost, Eloff, Oppose, Pentecost, UWC II, St. George, Kingston, Charge, Welcome, Special Synod, WCC Article, Oppose.

APARTHEID: Nobel, Oppose, Special Synod, UWC I, Epiphany, Christian Vision, Cape Press Club, Woodstock, Nobel, Special Synod, Nobel, UWC I, Nobel, UWC II, Woodstock, Oppose, Christianity and Crisis.

VIOLENCE AND NONVIOLENCE: Woodstock, Nobel, AAI Article, Woodstock, Times, Hope, Christianity and Crisis, Hope, Fighters, Fighters, Fighters, Fighters, UWC II, St. George, Cape Press Club, Cape Press Club.

FAMILY: Hope, Home, Nobel, Louisville, Crying, Crying, Crying, Nobel, Nobel, Hope, Nobel, Nobel, Fighters, Christianity and Crisis, New York, Crying, Home.

THE COMMUNITY—BLACK AND WHITE: Christianity and Crisis, Christian Vision, Christian Vision, Tutu, Hope, Oppose, Louisville, Tutu, Woodstock, UWC I, UWC II, Oppose, St. George, Woodstock, Black Sash, Tutu, Nobel.

TOWARD A NEW SOUTH AFRICA: Crying, Christianity and Crisis, Article, Hope, Times, UWC II, Crying, Crying, Crying, Biko, Natal I, New York, Crying, Nobel.

PHOTO CREDITS

p. 2   Portrait of Desmond Tutu in New York, 1984. (Jerry Soloway, UPI/Bettmann Newsphotos)

p. 20   Young African boy praying before a statue of a dark-skinned child Jesus in the Church of Christ the King, Johannesburg, 1955. (UPI/Bettmann)

p. 34   Black South African risks a fine of $20 or 20 days in prison for sitting on a "Europeans Only" bench, 1970. (UPI photo)

p. 44   Black student demonstrators in Leandra throw smoking teargas canisters back at police during a clash following the detention of 40 black youths by South African officials, 1985. (Reuters/Bettmann Newsphotos)

p. 54   Mother and son in Muthare Valley, a slum outside of Nairobi in Kenya, 1988. (Rex Miller)

p. 60   Two girls from Nairobi are fed through funds from a Western relief agency, 1988. (Rex Miller)

p. 68   A young black man, in an act of resistance, rides a bus restricted to whites in Durban, 1986. (Reuters/ Bettmann Newsphotos)

p. 80   Striking black mineworkers as they are bussed out of Vaal Reefs gold mine west of Johannesburg, 1987. (Wendy Schwegmann, Reuters/Bettmann Newsphotos)

p. 90   Relief worker in Muthare valley, Kenya, 1988. (Rex Miller)

p. 92   Tutu leads funeral march for four victims killed in clash with police in Dacluza, 1985. (Reuters/ Bettmann Newsphotos)

THE ACCLAIMED NEWMARKET *WORDS* SERIES

The Words of Desmond Tutu
Selected and Introduced by Naomi Tutu
Nearly 100 memorable quotations from the addresses, sermons, and writings of South Africa's Nobel Prize-winning Archbishop. Topics include: Faith and Responsibility, Apartheid, Family, Violence and Nonviolence, The Community—Black and White, and Toward a New South Africa. 10 photographs; chronology; text of acceptance speech for the Nobel Peace Prize, 1984. 112 pages, 5⅜ x 8. ISBN 1-55704-038-9. $12.95, hardcover.

The Words of Martin Luther King, Jr. Calendar
Quotations from letters, speeches, and writings, illustrated with inspirational, historical photographs. Highlights important events in Dr. King's life, North American holidays and astronomical data. For all ages. 10 X 12. Shrinkwrapped.

The Words of Martin Luther King, Jr.
Selected and introduced by Coretta Scott King
Over 120 quotations and excerpts from the great civil rights leader's speeches, sermons, and writings on: The Community of Man, Racism, Civil Rights, Justice and Freedom, Faith and Religion, Nonviolence, and Peace. 16 photos; chronology; text of presidential proclamation of King holiday. 128 pages, 5⅜ X 8. ISBN 0-937858-28-5, $10.95, hardcover. ISBN 0-937858-79-X, $7.95, paperback.

The Words of Gandhi
Selected and introduced by Richard Attenborough
Over 150 selections from the letters, speeches, and writings collected in five sections—Daily Life, Cooperation, Nonviolence, Faith, and Peace. 21 photographs; glossary. 112 pages. 5⅜ X 8. ISBN 0-937858-14-5, $10.95 hardcover.

The Words of Harry S Truman
Selected and introduced by Robert J. Donovan
This entirely new volume of quotations from Truman's speeches and writings gives the essence of his views on politics, leadership, civil rights, war and peace, and on "giving 'em hell." 15 photos; chronology. 112 pages. 5⅜ X 8. ISBN 0-937858-48-X, $9.95 hardcover.

The Words of Albert Schweitzer
Selected and introduced by Norman Cousins
An inspiring collection focusing on: Knowledge and Discovery, Reverence for Life, Faith, The Life of the Soul, The Musician as Artist, and Civilization and Peace. 22 photos; chronology. 112 pages. 5⅜ X 8. ISBN 0-937858-41-2, $9.95 hardcover.

More Inspirational Biography
Gandhi: A Pictorial Biography
Text by Gerald Gold, Photo Selection and Afterword by Richard Attenborough.
The important personal, political and spiritual periods of Gandhi's life. "First Rate"–LA Times. 150 photos; bibliography; map; index. 192 pages. 7¼ X 9. ISBN 0-937858-20-X, $9.95 paperback.

Available at your local bookseller or from Newmarket Press, 18 East 48th Street, New York, New York 10017, (212) 832-3575. Please add $1.50 per book or calendar for postage and handling, plus $.75 for each additional item ordered. (New York residents, please add applicable state and local sales tax.) Please allow 4–6 weeks for delivery. Prices and availability are subject to change. For information on quantity order discounts, please contact the Newmarket Special Sales Department.